D1315421

Keeping Unusual Pets

Rats

June McNicholas

Chicago, Illinois

www.heinemannraintree.com
Visit our website to find out more information about Heinemann-Raintree books.

To order:

☎ Phone 888-454-2279

▣ Visit www.heinemannraintree.com to browse our catalog and order online.

Edited by Louise Galpine, Megan Cotugno, and Laura Knowles
Designed by Kim Miracle and Ryan Frieson
Picture research by Mica Brancic
Originated by Capstone Global Library Ltd 2010
Printed and bound in China by Leo Paper Products Ltd

14 13 12 11 10
10 9 8 7 6 5 4 3 2 1

Library of Congress Cataloging-in-Publication Data
McNicholas, June, 1956-
  Rats / June McNicholas. -- 2nd ed.
    p. cm. -- (Keeping unusual pets)
  Originally published: 2003.
  Includes bibliographical references and index.
  ISBN 978-1-4329-3850-5 (hc)
  1. Rats as pets--Juvenile literature. [1. Rats as pets. 2. Pets.] I. Title.
  SF459.R3M36 2010
  636.935'2--dc22
                      2009035278

Acknowledgments
The author and publisher are grateful to the following for permission to reproduce copyright material: Ardea p. **20 bottom** (Johann de Meester); Bruce Coleman Collection pp. **7 top** (© Jane Burton), 42 (© Andrew Percell); © Capstone Global Library Ltd pp. **5, 8 top, 8 bottom, 9 top, 9 bottom, 11 top, 12, 14, 18 bottom, 19, 20 top, 22, 23 left, 23 right, 24, 25 bottom, 25 top, 26 left, 26 right, 27, 29 left, 29 right, 31 top, 31 bottom, 33, 35 top, 35 bottom, 37 top, 40** (Gareth Boden Photography), 43 (Maria Joannou), **16, 30, 34, 36, 37 bottom, 38, 41, 45 top, 45 bottom** (Tudor Photography); © Capstone Publishers pp. **15, 17, 18 top, 21, 28, 32 left, 32 right** (Karon Dubke); iStockphoto pp. **44 top** (© Alexander Novikov), **44 bottom** (© Dmitry Maslov); NHPA pp. **7** (© Stephen Dalton), 39 (© Daniel Heuclin); Science Photo Library pp. **5, 11, 13**; Shutterstock pp. **6** (krechet), **11 bottom** (Ragnarock).

Cover photograph of a rat reproduced with permission of Shutterstock (© Pakhnyushcha).

We would like to thank Judy Tuma and Rob Lee for their invaluable help in the preparation of this book.

Every effort has been made to contact copyright holders of material reproduced in this book. Any omissions will be rectified in subsequent printings if notice is given to the publisher.

Contents

Any words appearing in the text in bold, **like this**, are explained in the glossary.

What Is a Rat?

Most people think of rats as nasty wild animals that live in sewers and spread diseases. So, do not be surprised if people ask you how you could possibly want to have a rat as a pet!

But are pet rats really so horrible? The answer is, not a bit! Pet rats are not the same as wild rats that **scavenge**, or hunt for food, in garbage dumps or sewers. They have been **domesticated** for many years, so they now make excellent and friendly pets.

Many people think that rats are the best small pets for adults and children.

From the wild to our homes

Several centuries ago, people known as rat catchers were paid to kill **pest** rats. Eventually they started keeping unusually colored rats as pets and began **breeding** them. This was the beginning of the many color varieties of today's pet rats. In 1901 a lady asked if she could exhibit her pet rats at a show in England. Her black and white rat won "Best of Show." Since then, rats have become popular pets. A wild rat's life span is about one year, but domestic rats live for two to three years. This is because they are raised with good food, fresh water, and receive medical care.

FAMOUS RATS

One of the most famous pet rats was a white rat named Sammy. Sammy belonged to Beatrix Potter, the author of the Peter Rabbit stories.

Wild rats often live in garbage dumps. They survive by eating anything they can find.

NEED TO KNOW

✪ Wild rats are classed as **vermin**, or pests. It is **illegal** in many places to keep vermin as pets, so you must not take rats from the wild.

✪ Domesticated rats should not be allowed to breed with wild rats or be released into the wild.

✪ Children are not allowed to buy pets themselves. You should learn about pet rats and their care from a **breeder**, someone who already has a rat, reference books, and the Internet. Your family members must agree to bring a new pet into your home.

✪ Most countries have laws protecting animals. It is your responsibility to make sure your rats are healthy and well cared for. Always take your pets to the vet if they are sick or have been injured.

Rat Facts

Rats are **mammals**. This means they are **warm-blooded** (they produce their own body heat), give birth to their young, and feed their babies with their milk. They are members of the **rodent** family, which includes mice, rabbits, guinea pigs, hamsters, and gerbils. In fact, a lot of small pets are rodents!

All rodents have long teeth for gnawing. A rat's teeth grow throughout its life, so rats need to gnaw to keep their teeth short. If their teeth grow too long, they can die of starvation because they cannot eat properly.

Rats are members of the rodent family. Like all rodents, they will gnaw on things to keep their teeth short.

DID YOU KNOW?

- ✪ Rats live for around two to three years.
- ✪ Male rats are called **bucks**.
- ✪ Female rats are called **does**.
- ✪ The longest life span for a domestic rat was seven years and four months.
- ✪ There are rats that do not have fur. Those rats must be protected from extreme temperatures.
- ✪ France launched an astronaut rat into outer space in 1961.
- ✪ A rat's tail may be as long as its body.

Rat babies

Rats **mature**, or grow up, very quickly and can have babies of their own when they are only two or three months old. This is one reason why rats can be such **pests** in the wild. Rats have lots of babies in a **litter**. They can have several litters in a year, by which time the babies will have grown up enough to have babies of their own!

Clever climbers

Rats are fast-moving, **agile** creatures that are good at climbing. They are very intelligent and are good at solving problems. You can teach a rat to run through a maze to its food and it will remember which route is the quickest. Their intelligence is another reason why rats are pests in the wild—they can find food easily and can escape from humans and their traps—but it is also what makes rats very good pets.

Baby rats are called **kittens** or pups. When they are first born, they have no hair on their bodies and they cannot see.

Rats use their long tails to help them keep their balance.

Different colors

Pet rats come in lots of different colors. Colors for rats include white, cinnamon (reddish-brown), champagne (cream), chocolate (dark brown), and blue (smoky gray-blue). Rats of specific colors are grouped into types and are often called **fancy rats**. There are also rats that do not belong to a particular type, but they still look pretty and make good pets.

This picture shows a chocolate hooded rat (left) and a champagne hooded rat (right).

These rats are a silverthorn (left) and a chocolate rat (right).

A wide choice

There are lots of different types of fancy rat to choose from!
A good way to find out more about these varieties is to get in touch with a rat association or club—you can find details of a national association at the end of this book. You could also contact your local rat club, visit some rat shows, or talk to rat owners. You will soon find out that rats make excellent pets and are nothing like their wild cousins.

The rat above is a mink variegated rat.

This picture shows a Berkshire rat (top) and a hooded rat (bottom).

9

Are Rats for You?

Some people may tell you that rats make the best small pets of all because they are so intelligent and friendly. They might even think that they are more fun to own than cats or dogs.

As with all pets, there are good and bad things about owning rats. Here are some of the good points and not-so-good points.

GOOD POINTS

- Rats are intelligent. They recognize their owners and love human company.

- Rats will quickly learn your routine. You may find them waiting at the front of their cage when it is time for them to be taken out!

- Rats are not truly **nocturnal**, so they are happy to be up and active when you are.

- Rats are not expensive to buy or to feed.

- Above all, rats have character. They have big personalities in small bodies. This makes them real friends—some are more like little dogs or cats!

NOT-SO-GOOD POINTS

- A rat can bite hard if it is hurt or frightened.

- Rats will chew absolutely anything they can reach from their cage.

- Some **bucks** like to mark places where they have been with a few drops of **urine**. This does not smell, but it can be off-putting for some people.

- Sadly, rats do not live long. Most of them only live for about 24 to 30 months.

Yes or no?

So, are rats for you? Having rats for pets means giving them food and water every day, cleaning out their cage every week, and playing with them for about one hour every day. Are you really sure that you are prepared to do all these things, even when you are in a hurry or want to do something else? If the answer is "yes," then you could be ready to begin keeping rats as pets. This hobby could last for many years—or even for the rest of your life!

Your rats will love to sit on your shoulder. They will probably play with your hair and might even lick your face!

When your rats see you coming, they will run to the front of their cage—ready to play with you!

Choosing Your Rats

There are lots of things to think about when you are choosing a rat. Always take an adult with you to help you choose your pet, and if possible ask an experienced rat owner to also come along and give you advice.

One or more?

Rats like the company of other rats. It is not exactly wrong to own a single rat, but you will have to give your pet a lot of time and attention. A lone rat will probably be very unhappy.

It is much better to have two rats rather than one. They will be just as friendly with you, but they will also have each other for company when you are busy. In fact, two rats will be twice the fun! Try to choose two rats of the same age who are already used to each other. Best of all, choose two sisters or two brothers.

Rats are naturally **gregarious**. They enjoy playing with other rats.

Buck or doe?

Usually **bucks** are bigger than **does**. Bucks are also lazier, so they are probably the best choice if you want a pet that will sit quietly on your lap. The one drawback with bucks is that some of them like to mark the places they have been with a few drops of **urine**. This is a scent mark to let other rats know that your rat is around. We cannot smell it, but other rats can. It is less of a problem than it sounds, but some people do not like the idea very much.

TOP TIPS

- ✪ If you decide to own more than one rat, make sure that all your rats are the same sex. If they are not, you could end up with far more pets than you had planned for!

- ✪ Both bucks and does make equally good pets, so the choice is up to you.

- ✪ Try to visit some rat owners and rat shows to get to know a few bucks and does before you decide which will suit you best.

Does are usually more lively and playful than bucks. Most does do not mark places with urine, but a few of them (usually the very bossy ones!) do it just as much as bucks.

If you have two rats, they will keep each other company when you are not around.

What age?

It is best to choose pet rats that are about eight weeks old. Older rats take longer to get used to their human owners, and rats under six weeks are too young to leave their mothers. Unfortunately, many pet store owners will not know exactly how old their rats are, or even what sex they are. However, if you take experienced rat owners with you to help select your rats, they may be able to help.

These young rats look healthy and **alert**, with bright eyes and shiny coats. They would make excellent pets.

TOP TIP

Never buy a rat if it seems unwell or if its nose, eyes, ears, or rear end are not clean and free of discharge.

What to look for

There are a few basic things to look out for when you are choosing rats.

- ✪ The rats should be living in clean surroundings.
- ✪ They should be young, have bright eyes, and have clean noses, mouths, ears, and tails.
- ✪ Their coats should be soft and clean, with no sores or bald patches.
- ✪ They should be interested in you and settle down quickly when you hold them.

TOP TIP

If you are choosing a doe, make sure she has been separated from male rats since she was eight weeks old. Otherwise, she could be pregnant. It is unfair for an animal so young to **breed** when she is no more than a baby herself and still has a lot of growing up to do.

Your local rat **breeder** should have plenty of rats to choose from. Take a little time to get to know the rats before you choose any.

What Do I Need?

Rats can be kept in cages or tanks, but the most important thing is to give your pets plenty of room. Rats are active and playful creatures, and they will make good use of whatever space you provide.

Choosing a cage

Most people keep their pet rats in a cage. A cage measuring about 60 by 40 by 40 centimeters (24 by 16 by 16 inches) is about right for a pair of rats, but get a bigger one if you can.

Many pet stores stock cages especially for rats. Look for one that is roomy and easy to clean. Cages with metal bars and plastic trays in their base are simple to keep clean. Doors and cage panels need to be secure enough to prevent the rat from escaping, so test them carefully before you buy your cage.

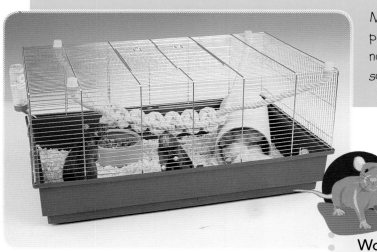

Most cages have metal bars and a plastic base. Make sure the bars are narrow enough to stop a rat from squeezing through!

TOP TIP

Wooden cages are not ideal. Rats will eventually gnaw them to pieces. They are difficult to keep clean as **urine** soaks into the wood, causing it to smell and rot.

Choosing a tank

Another place to keep rats is in a glass tank. However, it is very important to find a suitable lid for the tank. Choose one that lets in air but does not have large enough holes for your rats to climb through! It is very important to let enough air into the tank, because otherwise **condensation** (drops of water) can collect on the inside of the tank walls, making it damp. This can be dangerous to a rat's health.

TOP TIP

Rats love to climb, so choose a cage that is tall enough to fit ramps, ladders, ropes, or branches inside so that your rats can exercise and play.

There is plenty of space in this cage for climbing toys to keep your rats busy.

The perfect place

Once you have chosen your pets' home, you will need to find the right place for it. Rats can suffer from **heatstroke** if the temperature rises above 24°Celsius (75°Fahrenheit), so keep the cage out of direct sunlight and away from hot radiators. Rats can also become sick if the temperature drops below 7°C (45°F) or if they are kept in a draft. Choose a sheltered place for their cage where they will not be too hot or too cold, and where there is not much variation in temperature.

Wood shavings

You will need something to cover the floor of your rats' cage. Wood shavings are best. Make sure that you buy them from good pet stores rather than direct from a lumberyard. You do not want your wood shavings to be full of nails and splinters. Wood shavings from lumberyards may also contain germs from wild rats and mice that could make your pet rats sick.

Keep your cage on a table or shelf where the rats will not be bothered by other family pets.

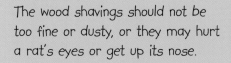

The wood shavings should not be too fine or dusty, or they may hurt a rat's eyes or get up its nose.

Bedding

Rats need material to make themselves a bed. You can use shredded paper for bedding, but avoid newspaper since the ink is not good for rats. Paper towels are fine—let the rats do the tearing up! Straw and hay are not suitable because they are not absorbent and do not get rid of smells.

TOP TIP

If good wood shavings are hard to find, try using cat litter pellets made from recycled paper. Some rat owners prefer to use these.

Bedding boxes

You may want to make a bedding box for your rats. A terracotta flower pot filled with bedding is fine. So is a cardboard shoe box with a rat-sized hole cut into its side. However, the rats will soon start chewing on the box. A bedding box will give your rats somewhere private to sleep. There are endless possibilities—you will find yourself looking at things and thinking, "I could give that to my rat to sleep in or play with."

Your rats will enjoy their comfortable sleeping box.

Toys for rats

Rats are playful and inquisitive creatures, so toys are a must. Your pets will enjoy having ladders and branches to climb on, shelves to run along, and tunnels to explore. Blocks of untreated and unpainted wood will give your rats something to chew on so they can keep their teeth short. Apple and pear wood are best. You can also buy chewing blocks from your pet store or rat **breeder**.

Blocks of wood are good for a rat's teeth and provide hours of chewing fun.

Climbing around

Many rat cages are fitted with shelves, ramps, and ladders, but you can also give your pets some branches to climb on. Choose dry, rough branches that are still covered with bark.

NOT TOO FULL!

Do not fill your pets' cage so full of toys that there is not enough room for them to run around! Most of all, rats enjoy plenty of open space.

Rats love climbing through, over, and under things!

Buying and making

Many pet stores and rat breeders sell colorful plastic tunnels, slides, and houses for rats to explore. You can also make your own rat toys from wide cardboard tubes and boxes with holes cut out of them. Try mixing up your pets' plastic toys with things you have made yourself to create an obstacle course. You could even try making a maze for your rats. Rats are so smart that your pets will soon find their way through the maze.

Your rats will have fun with almost anything you give them. But do not let your pets play with something they might swallow.

No wheels

Exercise wheels are not good for rats. They are often too small for adult rats, especially some of the hefty **bucks**. Wheels with open bars can be dangerous because rats' tails can get caught up in the bars and injured. Solid wheels are usually made of plastic, so rats will chew at them. Many plastic wheels have nasty metal spikes in the middle that are exposed once the plastic coating is gone. It is much better for your rats to have other toys to play with and to have lots of exercise time outside their cage.

Caring for Your Rats

Your rat cage will need to be cleaned out thoroughly once a week. Throw out all the wood shavings and bedding and wipe down the cage with a mild disinfectant. You can buy safe cleaning products from a pet store. Do not forget to wipe down the shelves as well as any toys or branches in the cage. When everything is thoroughly rinsed and completely dry, put in fresh wood shavings and bedding and put all the toys, branches, and shelves back inside the cage.

Rat **urine** can become quite smelly, so you and your family will soon notice if you do not clean the cage regularly!

A weekly cleaning does not take long and will keep your rats' home smelling fresh.

TOP TIP

You will not need to spend much time keeping your rats clean. Rats are naturally very clean animals and they spend a lot of time **grooming** themselves. However, rats' tails can sometimes get dirty. You can clean them with mild soap and water. Just rub the tail gently with a cloth, then rinse it with clean water.

Bath time

Rats rarely need baths, but they will need one if you decide to enter them in shows. If you treat your rats gently, bath times will not be stressful.

- ✪ Dip your rats into a bowl of lukewarm water and then hold them out of the water while you use a pet-safe shampoo on their coats and tails. Be careful not to let any shampoo get into their eyes or ears.

- ✪ Rinse your pets off in clean warm water and dry them with a towel. Talk softly and soothingly while you are doing this.

- ✪ Make sure your rats are completely dry and comfortable before they return to their cage.

DAILY CLEANING

In addition to giving the cage a weekly cleaning, you will also have some clearing up to do every day.

- ✪ Remove any uneaten food that is left scattered around the cage, especially fruits or vegetables that can attract flies.

- ✪ Wash the food bowl.

- ✪ Check the water bottle to make sure it is clean and fill it with fresh water.

- ✪ Remove any **feces** scattered about the cage.

- ✪ Scoop out any wood shavings made wet with urine.

- ✪ Rats can have an annoying habit of wetting their beds. Check that your rats' bedding is clean and dry.

Washing is easiest if you have two bowls, side by side—one for washing and the other for rinsing.

After you have dried your rats, they may like to scamper around a little to get warmed up!

Food for rats

Your rats' basic diet should be a mixture of grains and cereals that you can buy from a pet store. Rat food is sold in boxes or packages or even loose. However, make sure that the food is meant for rats. Gerbil and hamster food contains a lot of sunflower seeds and nuts, which rats love, but which can cause sore spots on a rat's skin. It is much better to feed your rats food made just for them, and give them an occasional sunflower seed or nut as a treat. Follow the feeding instructions on the package as a guideline for how much you should feed your pets.

Only feed your rats food that has been specially prepared for rats.

Healthy extras

You can add a few extra **ingredients** to your rats' basic diet. Whole-grain bread or toast, unsweetened breakfast cereals, cooked rice or noodles, and cooked potato will all be appreciated by your pets—but don't overdo it! Your rats will also enjoy chewing on a dog biscuit. This is a tasty way to keep their teeth healthy.

FRUITS AND VEGETABLES

Washed fruits and vegetables are good for rats. Start by giving your rats small amounts, to see which kinds they prefer.

✪ The best fruits are apples, although some rats love melon, cherries, and peaches! Do not feed your rats very acidic fruits such as oranges.

✪ Carrots, romaine lettuce, cabbage, and celery are good vegetables to give your rats.

✪ Do not feed onions or very strong-tasting vegetables to your pets.

Feeding times

You can choose when to feed your rats, but it is usually best to feed them in the evening, with a refill in the morning for breakfast if they need it. Rats will store extra food that they are not hungry enough to eat. Large amounts left over mean that you are overfeeding them!

Most rats love nibbling on fresh fruits and vegetables.

Rats are enthusiastic eaters! They often climb right inside their feeding bowl.

SAFETY FIRST

Rats can get stomachaches from eating too much fruit or too many vegetables. Stick to very small amounts and only give your rats fruits or vegetables every other day.

Tasty treats

You can buy various treats made especially for rats. These may be bars of cereals to be attached to the cage, tasty yogurt drops, or small cookies. Rats enjoy these, but you can offer them lots of other things, too. Your rats will almost certainly enjoy a small taste of cookie, chocolate, cake, or even ice cream—but do not give them too much! You know how bad it is to eat too much of these things, but your rats do not. A tiny taste now and then is okay, but it is up to you not to let your rats get fat or sick by eating too many of the wrong foods.

TOP TIP

Normally, if you like eating something, your rats will probably like it, too!

Your rats will probably love a small taste of ice cream, but never give them this much!

Pet stores sell a range of healthy treats like this.

A bony treat!

A good tasty treat for rats is a small, cooked bone with a little meat still on it. Rats enjoy meat, and chewing on the bone is good for their teeth. Bone can also provide valuable **calcium** that will help your pets to have strong teeth and bones. A clean, cooked bone can be left in the cage for a day or so, but meaty bones must be removed after one day, since they will soon go bad and start to smell.

Rats need to drink lots of water. Remember to fill their bottle with new, fresh water every day.

Water bottles

Finally, and very importantly, rats should always have fresh water to drink. A water bottle hung from the outside of the cage wires is best. You can also buy a clip to hang a water bottle from the lid of a tank. Water bottles work by letting drops of water flow whenever a rat licks the end of the spout. That way, your pets can get enough to drink without their bottle dripping into the cage.

VACATIONS

Rats need daily care. If you are going away, make sure you have arranged for someone to care for your pets.

- ✪ Ask a friend or neighbor who knows and likes rats.

- ✪ Show the person how much food to give your pets and how to change the water. If you will be gone a long time, show the person how to clean the cage.

- ✪ You should leave clear written instructions about how much to feed your pets, a phone number to reach you, and the vet's phone number.

Happy and healthy?

You need to check your pets regularly to make sure they are fit and well. Are your rats eating the proper amount and drinking regularly? Do they seem lively and **alert**? When you clean out the cage, check your rats' feces. They should not be very runny or too hard.

Daily checks

While you are handling your rats, feel them all over to make sure there are no lumps, bumps, or swellings on their bodies. Check that your pets' coats are clean and soft, with no sores or specks of dirt from fleas. Make sure that the skin on their ears and tails is clean and smooth, not rough and scaly.

TOP TIP

If you see something that could be a problem, tell your parents or another adult. They can help you decide whether you need to take your pet to the vet.

Look through each rat's fur to make sure there is no flea dirt.

28

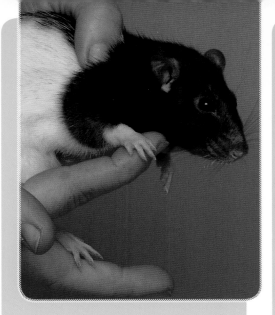

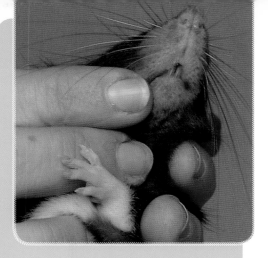

Check your rat's nails. If they are very long they should be trimmed.

This rat's teeth are the correct length. If your rat's teeth are longer than this, you will need to take your pet to the vet to have its teeth clipped.

Sometimes a rat's nails need trimming. Ask your vet to trim the nails to show you how to do it safely. Also, check your pets' teeth. Rats' teeth keep growing all the time, and if your pets are not chewing enough their teeth can become **overgrown**. If a rat's teeth become too long they can even stop it from feeding properly. You can find out more about health problems on pages 36 to 41.

WATCH OUT!

Here are some things to look out for when you are playing with your rats.

✪ Watch how your rats move around. A limp or an unusual way of walking may mean that your rat has been injured or is in pain.

✪ Are your pets getting fatter or thinner? A change in weight can be a sign of a serious health problem.

✪ Is one of your rats holding its head to one side? This may mean it has an ear problem.

Handling Your Rats

Pet rats are not wild animals. They have been **domesticated**, so they are happy to live with people. But this does not mean you will be able to handle your rats immediately. As with every friendship, human or animal, it will take a little time to get to know each other and feel confident together.

A new home

When you first take your rats home, give them time to settle in before you try to play with them or handle them.

Some rats settle in quicker than others. Some will be standing up at the bars demanding your attention as soon as they have explored their cage. Others will be quite shy and will have to be coaxed out of their cage. Food is always a great way to make friends! Quietly offer a tasty tidbit and let the rat take it from your fingers. If you have a very shy rat, you may need to put the treat near the front of the cage and sit quietly while it plucks up the courage to take it.

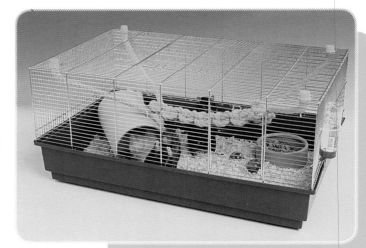

Your rats will probably take a while to explore their new home and settle in comfortably.

TOP TIP

Do not try to pick up your pets right away. Remember that your hand will look enormous to a rat, so it has to learn that you will not hurt it.

Take it slow

Take some time to allow your rats to get used to your voice and your hands. Your pets will have had a lot of changes in their short lives, and they will need to feel confident. Soon they will be taking food from you— first through the bars of their cage and then directly from your hand. They may even start putting their little

You will *seem like a giant to your rats! Talk to them softly and let them get used to the sound of your voice.*

feet on the palm of your hand while they take their food. This sort of confidence means that a rat is ready to be handled.

OTHER PETS

- ✪ You will need to be very careful about letting your rats meet other pets. Cats and dogs have the natural **instinct** to kill rats. Be careful when you introduce them and never leave them alone together.

- ✪ Rats can also frighten or even kill some other pets. Do not let them near hamsters or gerbils, even in their cages. It may be too upsetting for the smaller animal.

Your rats will *soon be happy to take a small piece of food from your fingers.*

Picking up your rat

Never pick up a rat by its tail. This is very frightening for your pet and may even injure it. Pick up a rat by putting one hand over its back and scooping it up into your other hand. This means that it will be sitting on one of your hands with your other hand over it. Stroke it and speak softly to it and try not to do anything too suddenly.

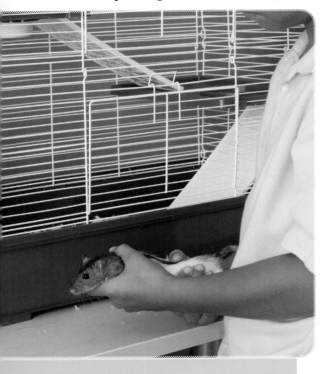

At first, a rat may not seem to like being handled, but it is important to hold it as much as you can so that it gets used to being held. Remember to always hold your rat with both hands. You need to be careful to stop it from accidentally falling or jumping.

Offer a treat, such as a little bit of ice cream on your fingers. Your pet will soon learn that handling means nice things are going to happen!

Be firm, gentle, and confident when you pick up your rat.

A rat will like being held against your body while you support its bottom with your other hand.

Contented chuckles

As your rats become more confident, let them sit on your shoulder. This is a favorite place for many rats, and they will happily sit with you while you watch TV or walk around the house. Often a happy rat will "chuckle" and make a tooth-grinding noise that can sound quite loud when it is right near your ear! Some rats even lick their owner's face. They have very soft, velvety tongues and very tickly whiskers!

TOP TIP

If your rats try to hide in your clothing, let them! Rats love being carried around in their owner's sweater or T-shirt, so it can be a good way of getting your pets used to riding around on you.

Playtime

You should spend some time every day playing with your rats outside of their cage. It is best to keep your rats in just one or two rooms where you can stay with them and make sure that they do not get into any trouble. You can give your pets some tubes and boxes to play in, but they will mainly enjoy just being out and exploring.

TOP TIP

You should always remember to wash your hands after handling a rat.

Your rat will love the new sights and scents outside of its cage.

Rat-proofing a room

Before you let your rats out to play, you will need to make sure that they cannot get hurt. You will also have to keep things safe from your rats! Be careful that there is nothing in their reach that they can chew to bits.

Inspect the room for any places where a rat could get stuck or lost. The best way to do this is to pretend to be a rat! Lie down flat on the floor and ask yourself what you can see that is rat-sized and might seem worth exploring. Look for gaps in walls, fireplaces, behind cabinets, or cracks in floorboards and under doors. These will all need to be blocked up. Check also that your pets cannot get inside furniture. A number of pet rats meet a sudden death by being sat on in sofas or chairs.

Before you let your rats out to play, make sure you cover any electric cables.

Electricity alert

Rats love chewing things. Electric cables and TV, video, and computer cords all look like tasty things for a rat to chew on. This could be very dangerous for your pet because it might get an electric shock that could kill it. If there are some cables that cannot be moved, fit protective cable sleeves around them to stop them from being chewed.

Chewing trouble

Rats can be very destructive if you are not careful. A favorite trick is to chew any material they can reach from their cage. Do not put clothing, papers, or other items near your pets' cage. They may reach out and drag them in! And if a rat disappears behind the curtains when it is out playing, it may be chewing holes in them!

If you leave anything close to your pets' cage, your rats will try to find a way to drag it inside!

Rats love objects that they can pick up and carry. Key rings, candy wrappers, pens, and even jewelry may all find their way into a rat's hiding place!

TOP TIPS

✪ Rats often steal things. This can be amusing, but rats are not smart enough to know when something is really harmful.

✪ Check your room to see what is lying around and remove any precious objects or things that would be bad for your rats to chew on.

Some Health Problems

Rats are healthy little animals, but there are a few illnesses and problems that rat owners need to recognize. Because rats are very small, they can get sick very fast—so having an experienced vet nearby is important.

Colds

Runny eyes and nose, wheezing, and sneezing may mean that your rat has a cold. Rats can catch colds if they are in a draft, if the temperature drops dramatically, or if they are near another rat with a cold. Sometimes the liquid from your rat's eyes and nose may be pink and look like blood, but it is not. Colds can be very serious to rats, so take your pet to the vet. The vet may give your pet medicine to help fight the cold. You must also keep it away from other rats to stop them from catching the cold, too. Make sure your rat is warm, drinking lots of water, and eating normally.

If your rat becomes seriously sick, take it straight to the vet.

Skin problems

Spots and sores on a rat's skin can be painful and itchy. There are two main causes of skin problems in rats. The first is diet. Your rat may have been eating too many sunflower seeds or nuts. If this is the case, replace its normal diet with very simple food for a few days, such as boiled rice and plain bread. If your rat's skin starts to look better, then diet was probably the cause.

The second cause of sores, scabs, and bald patches are **mites**. These are tiny **parasites** that live in some animals' coats. They may have come from hay or straw that they were in before you got them, or from another rat. If you have recently bought a new rat, you should ask your vet to check it for mites. If your pet has mites, your vet will give you a special shampoo to kill the mites. Change all the bedding and wood shavings in your pet's cage and do not let it near other rats until it is clear of mites.

STOMACH TROUBLES

✪ **Diarrhea** is often caused by too many fruits and vegetables or by too many unhealthy treats. This is easily fixed. Just feed your rat a very plain diet for a few days.

✪ Sometimes a rat can develop diarrhea if it is stressed from traveling or being moved from place to place. This normally settles down on its own.

✪ If your rat is suffering from **constipation** it will have very hard **feces** that are difficult to pass. Constipation can be very painful. It is often caused by too much dried food. Feeding your rat with a little lettuce and green leafy vegetables can improve things.

Normal rat feces should be quite soft and **cylindrical** in shape. If they are runny or very dry, your rat has a problem.

Ear problems

If your rat starts to hold its head tilted to one side, there is probably something wrong with its ears. Your rat may even have trouble balancing. Your vet will give you some ear drops to help clear the **infection**. Rats usually recover with a week or two of treatment.

Lumps and bumps

Many rats develop lumps and bumps. Sometimes these may be soft and full of **pus**. These are called **abscesses** and are caused by an infection developing around a wound or a bite. Abscesses can be drained and cleaned and usually heal very well.

Your vet will be able to give you advice about what to look for when examining your rats.

Other lumps may be firmer. Most of these lumps are **benign**, which means they are harmless. They can often be removed by an operation. Sadly, rats sometimes develop **cancerous tumors**. These often feel just like the benign lumps, but they grow fast and eventually make the rat very sick. If this happens, you should talk to your vet about whether it would be best to have your rat **put down**.

Tooth problems

A rat's teeth continue growing throughout its life, so your pets will need lots of hard things to gnaw on to wear down their teeth. Sometimes a rat's teeth can grow so long that it cannot eat properly and starts to lose weight. If this happens, your vet can clip your rat's teeth to the right length. Your rat will not like it, but it will not hurt.

A rat's teeth continue growing all the time. This rat has lost one of its upper teeth, so its lower tooth has not worn down and has grown extremely long.

TOP TIP

Make sure you give your pets lots of hard blocks of wood and other things to chew on to keep their teeth the right length.

EYE PROBLEMS

✪ If your rat has watery or runny eyes, ask an adult to help you bathe them with a soft tissue soaked in warm water. There may just be a speck of dust in your rat's eye.

✪ If the trouble comes back after bathing the eyes, it could be an infection. You will need to take your rat to the vet for some medicine.

Too hot

If your rats' cage is left in direct sunlight or too close to a hot radiator, your pets will become overheated and suffer from **heatstroke**. They will look uncomfortable and distressed, and their breathing will become rapid and shallow. Quickly move the cage to cooler surroundings and encourage your rats to drink cool water. If your rats collapse, wrap them in cool (not ice cold) damp towels and take them to the vet.

Too cold

If your rats become really cold, they may suffer from **hypothermia**. They will seem very slow and sluggish and may even collapse. Their bodies will be hunched over and feel cold to the touch. The best thing to do is to put your pets inside your shirt so your body temperature heats them up gently. If your rats do not show signs of getting better in 10 minutes, take them to the vet right away.

TOP TIP

If a rat becomes too cold, a little drink of warm milk or water will help to increase its body temperature.

If one of your rats develops hypothermia, you need to act fast. You could try taking it to a warm place and wrapping it up in a towel or blanket.

DANGER SIGNS

Watch out for these danger signs. They might mean that one of your rats is very sick.

- ✪ Your rat is sitting hunched over as if it is very uncomfortable. Its eyes may be half closed or it may be trembling. Its coat may look scruffy because it is not **grooming** itself.

- ✪ Your rat cannot walk without falling over. It may have a severe ear infection.

- ✪ Your rat has difficulty breathing and is gasping and wheezing. This may mean that the rat has **pneumonia**.

If your rat has any of these signs, you should contact your vet immediately.

If your rat is looking more scruffy than normal, it may be a sign that your pet is unwell.

Accidents can happen

Sometimes rats get broken legs. If this happens, you will need to take your pet to a vet very quickly. The vet will decide whether an operation is necessary to help mend the leg. Sometimes it may be necessary to **amputate** (cut off) a leg. Rats cope surprisingly well with only three legs. Occasionally a rat may have to be put down if its injuries are very serious.

In spite of these possible illnesses, you will probably find that your rats are healthy and active little creatures for most of their lives. However, a rat's life is short—only about two and a half years—so it will not be long before you have to think about your rat as an old animal.

Growing Old

Old rats need special care. They feel the cold more and are less active and **agile** than younger rats. It is a good idea to remove any ladders and climbing toys from their cage, as their balance may not be very good.

Give an old rat a quiet life with lots of gentle care and affection. It will still have a lot to enjoy in life, even if it is not as lively as it used to be. Even though it is old and slow, your rat will still be a friend who likes to sit on your shoulder.

Once a rat is over two years old, it will probably start to look old.

A peaceful end

Some old rats die peacefully in their sleep without ever becoming really sick. Others get lots of little illnesses, aches, and pains. These can mean that an old rat's life is no longer very enjoyable.

If your rat is old and sick and near the end of its life, you may decide that it is a good idea to talk to your vet about having it **put down**. The injection does not hurt—it just makes your pet feel sleepy. Before you can count to 10, your rat's heart will beat for the last time.

SAYING GOODBYE

It is hard to lose a pet that you have loved. It can seem very unfair that your rat has lived for such a short time. However, there are some things that you need to remember.

✪ It is not your fault, or the vet's fault, that your pet has died. It is just a hard fact that rats do not live long.

✪ When a pet dies, it is perfectly normal for people, adults as well as children, to cry for a while.

✪ Eventually the pain will pass, and you will be left with happy memories of your pet. Maybe you will soon think about getting another rat to care for and enjoy.

It can help to have a special burial place for your pet and to plant a flower or a shrub on it.

Keeping a Record

It is fun to keep a record of your pet rats. Buy a big scrapbook and fill it with notes and photos. Then you can look back at it and remind yourself of all the things you and your pets did together. Your rat scrapbook can also include general information about rats and how to care for them.

A special diary

Of course, pride of place in your scrapbook will go to your own rats. You could start with the very first photo taken of them when they came to live with you. Were they really those tiny **kittens**? Or what about the first time you held them? Or when they first sat on your shoulder? Or when Mom or Grandma were brave enough to hold them?

You can write down special events in the lives of your pets, such as the first time they explored your room or learned a funny trick. You can also make a note of the funny things your rats do when they are eating or playing.

Choosing which pictures to put in your scrapbook can be a lot of fun. Maybe you could ask other people which ones they like best, too.

Useful information

You can collect articles and information about rats and rat care and stick them into your scrapbook. They will soon build up into a good source of tips and guidance. You can also keep lists of your friends and contacts in rat clubs, the dates of shows, and useful websites about rats and how to care for them.

Rat shows

You may decide to show your rats. Groups such as the American **Fancy Rat** and Mouse Association encourage kids to get involved. Maybe your rats will win ribbons that you can keep in your scrapbook!

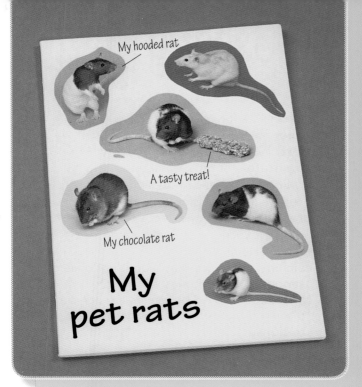

My hooded rat

A tasty treat!

My chocolate rat

My pet rats

When you have finished adding pictures to your scrapbook, it may be a good idea to label them. Otherwise, in years to come, you may forget what each picture is showing.

Your scrapbook should help to make sure that you never forget the special times that you and your rats enjoyed together.

Glossary

abscess soft lump filled with pus

agile able to move quickly and easily

alert lively and interested in everything

amputate cut off a leg or an arm

benign harmless or not dangerous

breed mate and produce young

breeder person who keeps animals to produce young

buck male rat

calcium substance that is good for building strong teeth and bones

cancerous caused by cancer. Cancer is a disease that destroys the body's healthy cells.

condensation water that collects as drops on a cold surface

constipation problem caused by hard feces that makes it difficult to go to the bathroom

cylindrical shaped like a tube

diarrhea runny feces

doe female rat

domesticate tame an animal so that it can live with people

fancy rat rat with special markings or colors, recognized as a particular type by rat associations

feces solid waste matter passed out of the body

gregarious sociable, or fond of company

groom clean an animal's coat; animals often groom themselves

heatstroke illness caused by getting too hot

hypothermia illness caused by getting too cold

illegal against the law

infection illness caused by germs

instinct natural tendency

ingredient part of a food or meal

kitten baby rat

litter group of baby rats born together

mammal animal with fur or hair on its body that feeds its babies with milk

mature become an adult

mite small creature that lives on another animal's skin and sucks its blood

nocturnal active at night

overgrown grown too long

parasite small creature such as a flea or worm that lives on or inside another animal

pest creature that causes problems for people, often by carrying diseases

pneumonia illness in which the lungs become infected and fill with fluid

pus thick yellow fluid inside an infected part of the body

put down give a sick animal an injection to help it die peacefully and without pain

rodent animal with strong front teeth for gnawing

scavenge hunt for food

tumor lump or growth

urine liquid passed out of the body containing water and waste substances

vermin animals that are pests, such as wild rats and mice

warm-blooded used to describe an animal that can keep its body at the same temperature

Find Out More

Books

There are not many books about rats written for young readers. Most of these books are not written specifically for children, but they can be enjoyed by rat owners of all ages:

Docommun, Debbie. *The Complete Guide to Rat Training.* Neptune City, N.J.: T. F. H., 2008.

Fields-Babineau, Miriam. *Rat Training: Complete Care and Training.* Irvine, Calif.: BowTie, 2009.

Mancini, Julie R. *Rats.* Neptune City, N.J.: T. F. H., 2009.

Waters, Jo. *The Wild Side of Pet Mice and Rats.* Chicago: Raintree, 2005.

Website

www.afrma.org
This is the website for the American Fancy Rat and Mouse Association. This group can provide you with lots of information about rats and how to care for them. They also have a calendar of rat shows throughout the country and a section just for kids.

Index